THIS PLANNER BELONGS TO:

_____

PHONE: _____

EMAIL _____

Copyright © 2024

Designed by Carolyn Wheeler and
Joanna Andrick
Publisher: Meaningful Thoughts, LLC
ISBN: 978-0-9976764-7-1
Publication Date: 2024
Edition: 1
Printed in the USA

All rights reserved. No part of this book may be reproduced, distributed, or transmitted in any form
or
by any means without the prior written permission of the publisher, except for brief quotations used in reviews or critiques.

THIS BOOK IS INTENDED FOR INFORMATIONAL PURPOSES ONLY. THE AUTHOR AND PUBLISHER MAKE NO REPRESENTATIONS OR WARRANTIES REGARDING THE ACCURACY, APPLICABILITY, OR COMPLETENESS OF THE CONTENTS OF THIS BOOK. THE INFORMATION PROVIDED IS NOT INTENDED TO REPLACE PROFESSIONAL MEDICAL, FINANCIAL, OR LEGAL ADVICE. READERS SHOULD SEEK PROFESSIONAL ASSISTANCE WHEN NEEDED. THE DESIGNERS AND PUBLISHER DISCLAIM ANY LIABILITY OR RESPONSIBILITY TO ANY PERSON OR ENTITY FOR ANY LOSS OR DAMAGE CAUSED OR ALLEGED TO BE CAUSED, DIRECTLY OR INDIRECTLY, BY THE INFORMATION CONTAINED IN THIS BOOK.

Daisy's Place™ The Thriving Caregiver™ Thriving Caregiver™ Caregivers helping caregivers™ The heart of our community.

For More Thriving Caregiver™ Resources Go To ThrivingCaregiver.com

Introduction

Welcome to your planner!

Caring for a loved one is a journey filled with both blessings and challenges, and this planner is here to support you every step of the way. As a caregiver, you manage so much more than a typical schedule, you're balancing routines, appointments, medications, and countless details that require both patience and resilience. This planner is designed especially for you, offering a place to organize, reflect, and track the essential aspects of your caregiving role.

If there's more than one caregiver involved, this planner becomes even more invaluable. When shifts change or new helpers step in, the details of the day often get lost. This planner is your source of information, so every caregiver involved can go straight here to see what has transpired, what's coming up, and what still needs attention. It's a time-saver and a comfort, a reliable place to keep everything organized, allowing you to avoid chaos and stay grounded. In many ways, this planner is a lifeline, ensuring that nothing important slips through the cracks.

Just as important as tracking the details of caregiving, though, is remembering to take care of yourself. As you pour out your time, energy, and love for others, it's essential to nurture your own well-being, too. This planner encourages you to prioritize self-care, even in small moments, so you can remain strong and resilient for those you care for. Alongside this planner, you may also find support in our companion The Thriving Caregiver book, and two Thriving Caregiver's Journals, available at www.thrivingcaregiver.com, which offers space for reflection and peace.

Within these pages, you'll find tools not only to keep track of daily routines but also to manage the unexpected, set personal goals, and find reminders of the importance of self-care. From scheduling appointments to noting important details about your loved one's care, this planner is your companion in staying organized and feeling prepared. May it bring you a little extra peace and clarity, empowering you to care for others with grace while still nurturing yourself.

Thank you for your dedication and compassion. Here's to a year of purpose, strength, and support as you navigate this unique journey.

Love,
Carolyn

The Thriving Planner

Advice Column

Track Symptoms in Real Time:

Record symptoms as they occur to spot patterns and provide clear info at doctor visits.

Organize Medical Information

Store critical records and appointment notes in the "Important Documents" section for quick access.

Make It Personal

Add notes, prayers, or affirmations that inspire and support you on this journey.

Remember the remedy!

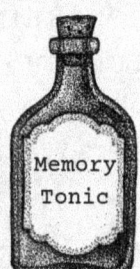

Be a Thriving Caregiver and plan every dose!

Set Weekly Goals:

Begin each week with a small, achievable goal—like a daily break or connecting with a friend.

A Penny for your thoughts?

Never be late again!

Weekly Questions:

Reflections to nurture your well-being.

Use the 5th Week for Flexibility:

If you don't need the 5th week, in a month repurpose it for notes, habit tracking, or unique caregiving reminders.

Important Documents

Medical:
- [ ] All Medical Records
- [ ] Health Insurance Card
- [ ] Advanced Health Care Directive
- [ ] Living Will
- [ ] HIPAA Form
- [ ] Power of Attorney
- [ ] End of life arrangements

Legal:
- [ ] Will or Trust
- [ ] Guardianship Documents
- [ ] Property and Asset Documentation
- [ ] Driver's License
- [ ] HIPAA Form
- [ ] Birth Certificate
- [ ] Social Security Card

Financial:
- [ ] Income Sources
- [ ] Tax Records
- [ ] Retirement Account Information
- [ ] Insurance Policies
- [ ] Credit Card
- [ ] Loan Information
- [ ] Rent & Utilities

Additional Documents
- [ ]
- [ ]
- [ ]
- [ ]

Legal:
- [ ] Emergency Contact List
- [ ] Online Login Information
- [ ] Friends and Family Contact Information

Contacts

NAME: _____
PHONE: _____
INFO: _____
_____

NAME: _____
PHONE: _____
INFO: _____
_____

NAME: _____
PHONE: _____
INFO: _____
_____

NAME: _____
PHONE: _____
INFO: _____
_____

NAME: _____
PHONE: _____
INFO: _____
_____

NAME: _____
PHONE: _____
INFO: _____
_____

NAME: _____
PHONE: _____
INFO: _____
_____

NAME: _____
PHONE: _____
INFO: _____
_____

NAME: _____
PHONE: _____
INFO: _____
_____

NAME: _____
PHONE: _____
INFO: _____
_____

Contacts

NAME: _____
PHONE: _____
INFO: _____
_____

NAME: _____
PHONE: _____
INFO: _____
_____

NAME: _____
PHONE: _____
INFO: _____
_____

NAME: _____
PHONE: _____
INFO: _____
_____

NAME: _____
PHONE: _____
INFO: _____
_____

NAME: _____
PHONE: _____
INFO: _____
_____

NAME: _____
PHONE: _____
INFO: _____
_____

NAME: _____
PHONE: _____
INFO: _____
_____

NAME: _____
PHONE: _____
INFO: _____
_____

NAME: _____
PHONE: _____
INFO: _____
_____

Month of:

Sunday	Monday	Tuesday	Wednesday	Thursday	Friday	Saturday

Notes:
_____
_____
_____
_____
_____
_____

At a Glance:

MEDICAL APPOINTMENTS

- [ ]
- [ ]
- [ ]
- [ ]
- [ ]
- [ ]
- [ ]
- [ ]
- [ ]
- [ ]
- [ ]
- [ ]

PERSCRIPTIONS AND SUPPLIES

- [ ]
- [ ]
- [ ]
- [ ]
- [ ]
- [ ]
- [ ]
- [ ]
- [ ]
- [ ]
- [ ]
- [ ]

EVENTS

NEEDS

TO-DO

Caregiver Self-Care

What made me smile this week?

Did I nourish my body well this week?

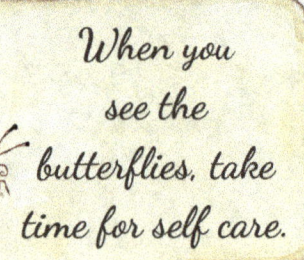

When you see the butterflies, take time for self care.

How can I reconnect with my faith this week?

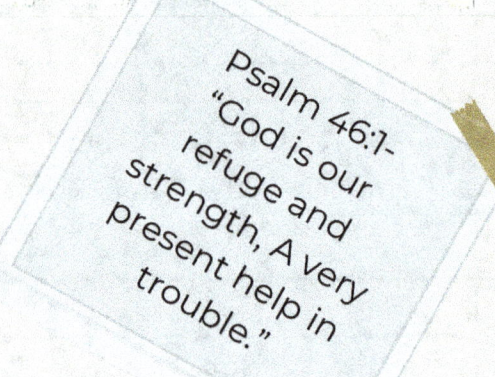

Psalm 46:1- "God is our refuge and strength, A very present help in trouble."

What brought me joy this week?

Medication Map

Medication: Medication:

Dose: Dose:

Frequency: Frequency:

Time: Time:

Medication: Medication:

Dose: Dose:

Frequency: Frequency:

Time: Time:

Medication: Medication:

Dose: Dose:

Frequency: Frequency:

Time: Time:

Medication: Medication:

Dose: Dose:

Frequency: Frequency:

Time: Time:

Medication: Medication:

Dose: Dose:

Frequency: Frequency:

Time: Time:

| Sunday | Monday | Tuesday | Wednesday |

MEDICATION TRACKING

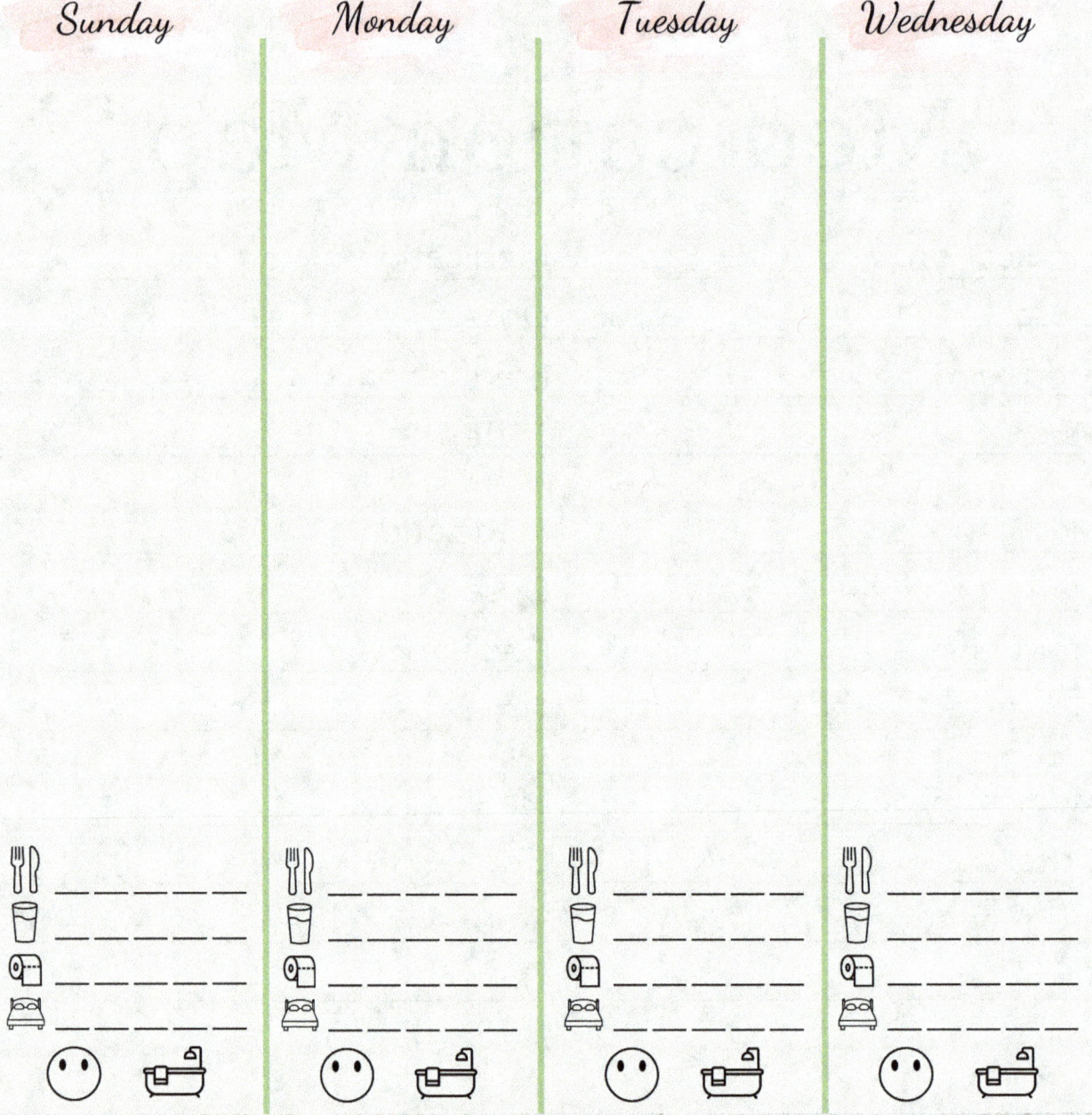

Thursday	Friday	Saturday	Reflections
			What made me smile this week?

SYMPTOM TRACKING

Sunday	Monday	Tuesday	Wednesday

MEDICATION TRACKING

Thursday	Friday	Saturday	Reflections

Did I nourish my body well this week?

SYMPTOM TRACKING

Sunday	Monday	Tuesday	Wednesday

MEDICATION TRACKING

Thursday	Friday	Saturday	Reflections

How can I reconnect with my faith this week?

SYMPTOM TRACKING

Sunday	Monday	Tuesday	Wednesday

MEDICATION TRACKING

Thursday	Friday	Saturday	Reflections
			What brought me joy this week?

SYMPTOM TRACKING

| Sunday | Monday | Tuesday | Wednesday |

MEDICATION TRACKING

Thursday	Friday	Saturday	Reflections

Psalm 46:1- "God is our refuge and strength. A very present help in trouble."

SYMPTOM TRACKING

Month of:

Sunday	Monday	Tuesday	Wednesday	Thursday	Friday	Saturday

Notes:

At a Glance:

MEDICAL APPOINTMENTS

- [ ]
- [ ]
- [ ]
- [ ]
- [ ]
- [ ]
- [ ]
- [ ]
- [ ]
- [ ]
- [ ]

EVENTS

PERSCRIPTIONS AND SUPPLIES

- [ ]
- [ ]
- [ ]
- [ ]
- [ ]
- [ ]
- [ ]
- [ ]
- [ ]
- [ ]
- [ ]

NEEDS

TO-DO

Caregiver Self-Care

How can I celebrate a small win?

How can I rest more fully tonight?

When you see the butterflies, take time for self care.

What can I pray about today?

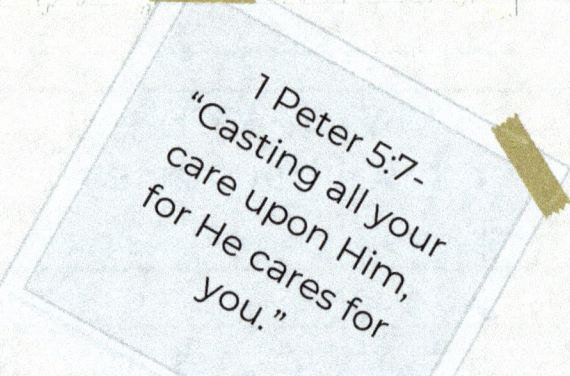

1 Peter 5:7 - "Casting all your care upon Him, for He cares for you."

What is one small thing I can do for myself?

Medication Map

Medication: | Medication:
Dose: | Dose:
Frequency: | Frequency:
Time: | Time:

Medication: | Medication:
Dose: | Dose:
Frequency: | Frequency:
Time: | Time:

Medication: | Medication:
Dose: | Dose:
Frequency: | Frequency:
Time: | Time:

Medication: | Medication:
Dose: | Dose:
Frequency: | Frequency:
Time: | Time:

Medication: | Medication:
Dose: | Dose:
Frequency: | Frequency:
Time: | Time:

Sunday | Monday | Tuesday | Wednesday

MEDICATION TRACKING

| Thursday | Friday | Saturday | Reflections |

How can I celebrate a small win?

SYMPTOM TRACKING

| Sunday | Monday | Tuesday | Wednesday |

MEDICATION TRACKING

Thursday	Friday	Saturday	Reflections

How can I rest more fully tonight?

SYMPTOM TRACKING

Sunday	Monday	Tuesday	Wednesday

MEDICATION TRACKING

Thursday | Friday | Saturday | Reflections

What can I pray about today?

SYMPTOM TRACKING

| Sunday | Monday | Tuesday | Wednesday |

MEDICATION TRACKING

Thursday	Friday	Saturday	Reflections

What is one small thing I can do for myself?

SYMPTOM TRACKING

| Sunday | Monday | Tuesday | Wednesday |

MEDICATION TRACKING

Thursday	Friday	Saturday	Reflections

1 Peter 5:7 – "Casting all your care upon Him, for He cares for you."

SYMPTOM TRACKING

Month of:

Sunday	Monday	Tuesday	Wednesday	Thursday	Friday	Saturday

Notes:

At a Glance:

MEDICAL APPOINTMENTS

- [ ]
- [ ]
- [ ]
- [ ]
- [ ]
- [ ]
- [ ]
- [ ]
- [ ]
- [ ]
- [ ]

PERSCRIPTIONS AND SUPPLIES

- [ ]
- [ ]
- [ ]
- [ ]
- [ ]
- [ ]
- [ ]
- [ ]
- [ ]
- [ ]

EVENTS

NEEDS

TO-DO

Caregiver Self-Care

What can I let go of that isn't helping me?

What movement or exercise feels good to me?

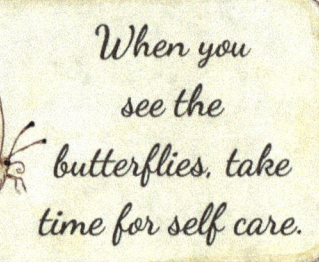

When you see the butterflies, take time for self care.

What inspires me to feel hopeful?

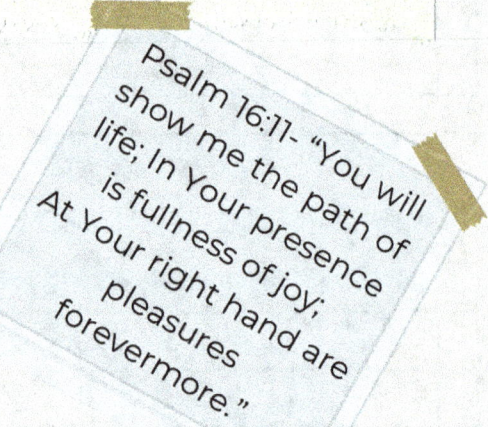

Psalm 16:11- "You will show me the path of life; In Your presence is fullness of joy; At Your right hand are pleasures forevermore."

How can I make time for relaxation?

Medication Map

Medication: Medication:

Dose: Dose:

Frequency: Frequency:

Time: Time:

Medication: Medication:

Dose: Dose:

Frequency: Frequency:

Time: Time:

Medication: Medication:

Dose: Dose:

Frequency: Frequency:

Time: Time:

Medication: Medication:

Dose: Dose:

Frequency: Frequency:

Time: Time:

Medication: Medication:

Dose: Dose:

Frequency: Frequency:

Time: Time:

Sunday | Monday | Tuesday | Wednesday

MEDICATION TRACKING

Thursday   Friday   Saturday   Reflections

What can I let go of that isn't helping me?

SYMPTOM TRACKING

Sunday	Monday	Tuesday	Wednesday

MEDICATION TRACKING

Thursday | Friday | Saturday | Reflections

What movement or exercise feels good to me?

SYMPTOM TRACKING

Sunday | Monday | Tuesday | Wednesday

MEDICATION TRACKING

Thursday	Friday	Saturday	Reflections

What inspires me to feel hopeful?

SYMPTOM TRACKING

Sunday	Monday	Tuesday	Wednesday

MEDICATION TRACKING

Thursday	Friday	Saturday	Reflections
			How can I make time for relaxation?

SYMPTOM TRACKING

Sunday	Monday	Tuesday	Wednesday

MEDICATION TRACKING

Thursday

Friday

Saturday

Reflections

Psalm 16:11- "You will show me the path of life; In Your presence is fullness of joy; At Your right hand are pleasures forevermore."

SYMPTOM TRACKING

Month of:

Sunday	Monday	Tuesday	Wednesday	Thursday	Friday	Saturday

Notes:

At a Glance:

MEDICAL APPOINTMENTS

- [ ]
- [ ]
- [ ]
- [ ]
- [ ]
- [ ]
- [ ]
- [ ]
- [ ]
- [ ]
- [ ]

PERSCRIPTIONS AND SUPPLIES

- [ ]
- [ ]
- [ ]
- [ ]
- [ ]
- [ ]
- [ ]
- [ ]
- [ ]
- [ ]
- [ ]

EVENTS

NEEDS

TO-DO

Caregiver Self-Care

What is one thing I can be grateful for?

What healthy habit can I build this week?

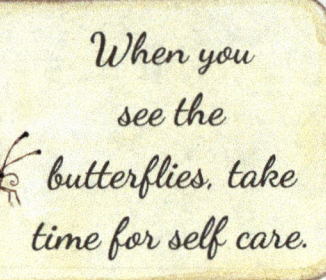

When you see the butterflies, take time for self care.

How can I express gratitude in my life?

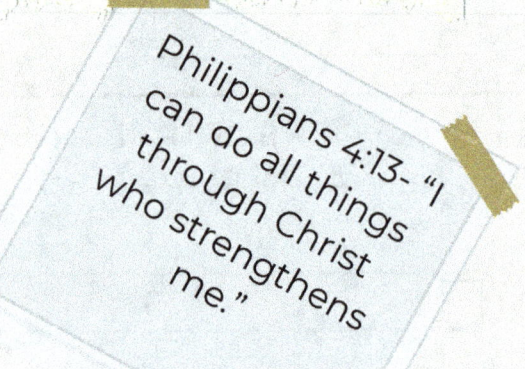

Philippians 4:13- "I can do all things through Christ who strengthens me."

What activity helps me recharge?

Medication Map

Medication:	Medication:
Dose:	Dose:
Frequency:	Frequency:
Time:	Time:
Medication:	Medication:
Dose:	Dose:
Frequency:	Frequency:
Time:	Time:
Medication:	Medication:
Dose:	Dose:
Frequency:	Frequency:
Time:	Time:
Medication:	Medication:
Dose:	Dose:
Frequency:	Frequency:
Time:	Time:
Medication:	Medication:
Dose:	Dose:
Frequency:	Frequency:
Time:	Time:

| Sunday | Monday | Tuesday | Wednesday |

MEDICATION TRACKING

Thursday

Friday

Saturday

Reflections

What is one thing I can be grateful for?

SYMPTOM TRACKING

Sunday	Monday	Tuesday	Wednesday

MEDICATION TRACKING

| Thursday | Friday | Saturday | Reflections |

What healthy habit can I build this week?

SYMPTOM TRACKING

| Sunday | Monday | Tuesday | Wednesday |

MEDICATION TRACKING

Thursday	Friday	Saturday	Reflections

How can I express gratitude in my life?

SYMPTOM TRACKING

| Sunday | Monday | Tuesday | Wednesday |

MEDICATION TRACKING

| Thursday | Friday | Saturday | Reflections |

What activity helps me recharge?

SYMPTOM TRACKING

| Sunday | Monday | Tuesday | Wednesday |

MEDICATION TRACKING

Thursday	Friday	Saturday	Reflections

Philippians 4:13- "I can do all things through Christ who strengthens me."

SYMPTOM TRACKING

Month of:

Sunday	Monday	Tuesday	Wednesday	Thursday	Friday	Saturday

Notes:

At a Glance:

MEDICAL APPOINTMENTS

- [ ] _____
- [ ] _____
- [ ] _____
- [ ] _____
- [ ] _____
- [ ] _____
- [ ] _____
- [ ] _____
- [ ] _____
- [ ] _____
- [ ] _____

PERSCRIPTIONS AND SUPPLIES

- [ ] _____
- [ ] _____
- [ ] _____
- [ ] _____
- [ ] _____
- [ ] _____
- [ ] _____
- [ ] _____
- [ ] _____
- [ ] _____

EVENTS

_____
_____
_____
_____
_____
_____

NEEDS

TO-DO

Caregiver Self-Care

How can I set boundaries to protect my energy?

How can I make my meals more enjoyable?

When you see the butterflies, take time for self care.

What Bible verse or quote can I reflect on?

Psalm 46:10- "Be still, and know that I am God; I will be exalted among the nations, I will be exalted in the earth!"

Who can I reach out to for support this week?

Medication Map

Medication: _____

Dose: _____

Frequency: _____

Time: _____

Medication: _____

Dose: _____

Frequency: _____

Time: _____

Medication: _____

Dose: _____

Frequency: _____

Time: _____

Medication: _____

Dose: _____

Frequency: _____

Time: _____

Medication: _____

Dose: _____

Frequency: _____

Time: _____

Medication: _____

Dose: _____

Frequency: _____

Time: _____

Medication: _____

Dose: _____

Frequency: _____

Time: _____

Medication: _____

Dose: _____

Frequency: _____

Time: _____

Sunday	Monday	Tuesday	Wednesday

MEDICATION TRACKING

Thursday	Friday	Saturday	Reflections

How can I set boundaries to protect my energy?

SYMPTOM TRACKING

| Sunday | Monday | Tuesday | Wednesday |

MEDICATION TRACKING

Thursday

Friday

Saturday

Reflections

How can I make my meals more enjoyable?

SYMPTOM TRACKING

Sunday	Monday	Tuesday	Wednesday

MEDICATION TRACKING

Thursday	Friday	Saturday	Reflections

What Bible verse or quote can I reflect on?

SYMPTOM TRACKING

Sunday	Monday	Tuesday	Wednesday

MEDICATION TRACKING

Thursday	Friday	Saturday	Reflections

Who can I reach out to for support this week?

SYMPTOM TRACKING

Sunday	Monday	Tuesday	Wednesday

MEDICATION TRACKING

Thursday

Friday

Saturday

Reflections

Psalm 46:10- "Be still, and know that I am God; I will be exalted among the nations, I will be exalted in the earth!"

SYMPTOM TRACKING

Month of:

Sunday	Monday	Tuesday	Wednesday	Thursday	Friday	Saturday

Notes:

At a Glance:

MEDICAL APPOINTMENTS

- [ ] _____
- [ ] _____
- [ ] _____
- [ ] _____
- [ ] _____
- [ ] _____
- [ ] _____
- [ ] _____
- [ ] _____
- [ ] _____
- [ ] _____

PERSCRIPTIONS AND SUPPLIES

- [ ] _____
- [ ] _____
- [ ] _____
- [ ] _____
- [ ] _____
- [ ] _____
- [ ] _____
- [ ] _____
- [ ] _____
- [ ] _____
- [ ] _____

EVENTS

_____
_____
_____
_____
_____

NEEDS

TO-DO

Caregiver Self-Care

What did I learn about myself this week?

Did I drink enough water today?

When you see the butterflies, take time for self care.

How can I serve others with a joyful heart?

Matthew 11:28- "Come to Me, all you who labor and are heavy laden, and I will give you rest."

What helps me feel calm during stress?

Medication Map

Medication:	Medication:
Dose:	Dose:
Frequency:	Frequency:
Time:	Time:
Medication:	Medication:
Dose:	Dose:
Frequency:	Frequency:
Time:	Time:
Medication:	Medication:
Dose:	Dose:
Frequency:	Frequency:
Time:	Time:
Medication:	Medication:
Dose:	Dose:
Frequency:	Frequency:
Time:	Time:
Medication:	Medication:
Dose:	Dose:
Frequency:	Frequency:
Time:	Time:

Sunday	Monday	Tuesday	Wednesday

MEDICATION TRACKING

Thursday	Friday	Saturday	Reflections

What did I learn about myself this week?

SYMPTOM TRACKING

| Sunday | Monday | Tuesday | Wednesday |

MEDICATION TRACKING

Thursday	Friday	Saturday	Reflections

Did I drink enough water today?

SYMPTOM TRACKING

Sunday | Monday | Tuesday | Wednesday

MEDICATION TRACKING

Thursday

Friday

Saturday

Reflections

How can I serve others with a joyful heart?

SYMPTOM TRACKING

| Sunday | Monday | Tuesday | Wednesday |

MEDICATION TRACKING

Thursday	Friday	Saturday	Reflections

What helps me feel calm during stress?

SYMPTOM TRACKING

| Sunday | Monday | Tuesday | Wednesday |

MEDICATION TRACKING

Thursday

Friday

Saturday

Reflections

Matthew 11:28- "Come to Me, all you who labor and are heavy laden, and I will give you rest."

SYMPTOM TRACKING

Month of:

Sunday	Monday	Tuesday	Wednesday	Thursday	Friday	Saturday

Notes:

At a Glance:

MEDICAL APPOINTMENTS

- [ ] _____
- [ ] _____
- [ ] _____
- [ ] _____
- [ ] _____
- [ ] _____
- [ ] _____
- [ ] _____
- [ ] _____
- [ ] _____
- [ ] _____

PERSCRIPTIONS AND SUPPLIES

- [ ] _____
- [ ] _____
- [ ] _____
- [ ] _____
- [ ] _____
- [ ] _____
- [ ] _____
- [ ] _____
- [ ] _____
- [ ] _____

EVENTS

_____
_____
_____
_____
_____
_____

NEEDS

TO-DO

Caregiver Self-Care

How can I show kindness to myself today?

How can I support my body tomorrow?

When you see the butterflies, take time for self care.

What brings me closer to God this week?

Isaiah 40:31- "But those who wait on the Lord Shall renew their strength..."

How can I adjust my expectations of myself?

Medication Map

Medication:	Medication:
Dose:	Dose:
Frequency:	Frequency:
Time:	Time:
Medication:	Medication:
Dose:	Dose:
Frequency:	Frequency:
Time:	Time:
Medication:	Medication:
Dose:	Dose:
Frequency:	Frequency:
Time:	Time:
Medication:	Medication:
Dose:	Dose:
Frequency:	Frequency:
Time:	Time:
Medication:	Medication:
Dose:	Dose:
Frequency:	Frequency:
Time:	Time:

Sunday | Monday | Tuesday | Wednesday

MEDICATION TRACKING

Thursday	Friday	Saturday	Reflections

How can I show kindness to myself today?

SYMPTOM TRACKING

Sunday | Monday | Tuesday | Wednesday

MEDICATION TRACKING

| Thursday | Friday | Saturday | Reflections |

How can I support my body tomorrow?

SYMPTOM TRACKING

Sunday | Monday | Tuesday | Wednesday

MEDICATION TRACKING

Thursday | Friday | Saturday | Reflections

What brings me closer to God this week?

SYMPTOM TRACKING

Sunday　　　　　Monday　　　　　Tuesday　　　　　Wednesday

MEDICATION TRACKING

Thursday | Friday | Saturday | Reflections

How can I adjust my expectations of myself?

SYMPTOM TRACKING

Sunday | Monday | Tuesday | Wednesday

MEDICATION TRACKING

Thursday   Friday   Saturday   Reflections

Isaiah 40:31- "But those who wait on the Lord Shall renew their strength..."

SYMPTOM TRACKING

Month of:

Sunday	Monday	Tuesday	Wednesday	Thursday	Friday	Saturday

Notes:

At a Glance:

MEDICAL APPOINTMENTS

- ☐ _____
- ☐ _____
- ☐ _____
- ☐ _____
- ☐ _____
- ☐ _____
- ☐ _____
- ☐ _____
- ☐ _____
- ☐ _____
- ☐ _____

PERSCRIPTIONS AND SUPPLIES

- ☐ _____
- ☐ _____
- ☐ _____
- ☐ _____
- ☐ _____
- ☐ _____
- ☐ _____
- ☐ _____
- ☐ _____
- ☐ _____
- ☐ _____

EVENTS

_____
_____
_____
_____
_____

NEEDS

TO-DO

Caregiver Self-Care

What thought can I focus on for peace?

What is one physical activity I can enjoy?

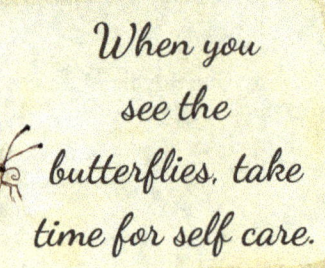

When you see the butterflies, take time for self care.

How can I find quiet moments to reflect?

John 16:33- "These things I have spoken to you, that in Me you may have peace... be of good cheer, I have overcome the world."

What is something I can do to pamper myself?

Medication Map

Medication:	Medication:
Dose:	Dose:
Frequency:	Frequency:
Time:	Time:
Medication:	Medication:
Dose:	Dose:
Frequency:	Frequency:
Time:	Time:
Medication:	Medication:
Dose:	Dose:
Frequency:	Frequency:
Time:	Time:
Medication:	Medication:
Dose:	Dose:
Frequency:	Frequency:
Time:	Time:
Medication:	Medication:
Dose:	Dose:
Frequency:	Frequency:
Time:	Time:

| Sunday | Monday | Tuesday | Wednesday |

MEDICATION TRACKING

Thursday

Friday

Saturday

Reflections

What thought can I focus on for peace?

SYMPTOM TRACKING

Sunday	Monday	Tuesday	Wednesday

MEDICATION TRACKING

Thursday	Friday	Saturday	Reflections
			What is one physical activity I can enjoy?

SYMPTOM TRACKING

Sunday	Monday	Tuesday	Wednesday

MEDICATION TRACKING

Thursday	Friday	Saturday	Reflections
			🦋 How can I find quiet moments to reflect?

SYMPTOM TRACKING

Sunday	Monday	Tuesday	Wednesday

MEDICATION TRACKING

Thursday	Friday	Saturday	Reflections

What is something I can do to pamper myself?

SYMPTOM TRACKING

Sunday	Monday	Tuesday	Wednesday

MEDICATION TRACKING

| Thursday | Friday | Saturday | Reflections |

John 16:33- "These things I have spoken to you, that in Me you may have peace... be of good cheer, I have overcome the world."

SYMPTOM TRACKING

Month of:

Sunday	Monday	Tuesday	Wednesday	Thursday	Friday	Saturday

Notes:
_____
_____
_____
_____
_____
_____

At a Glance:

MEDICAL APPOINTMENTS

- [ ] _____
- [ ] _____
- [ ] _____
- [ ] _____
- [ ] _____
- [ ] _____
- [ ] _____
- [ ] _____
- [ ] _____
- [ ] _____
- [ ] _____

PERSCRIPTIONS AND SUPPLIES

- [ ] _____
- [ ] _____
- [ ] _____
- [ ] _____
- [ ] _____
- [ ] _____
- [ ] _____
- [ ] _____
- [ ] _____
- [ ] _____
- [ ] _____

EVENTS

_____
_____
_____
_____
_____
_____

NEEDS

TO-DO

Caregiver Self-Care

How can I simplify my to-do list?

How can I prioritize sleep this week?

When you see the butterflies, take time for self care.

What reminds me of my purpose in caregiving?

Psalm 55:22- "Cast your burden on the Lord, And He shall sustain you; He shall never permit the righteous to be moved."

How can I make next week more manageable?

Medication Map

Medication: Medication:

Dose: Dose:

Frequency: Frequency:

Time: Time:

Medication: Medication:

Dose: Dose:

Frequency: Frequency:

Time: Time:

Medication: Medication:

Dose: Dose:

Frequency: Frequency:

Time: Time:

Medication: Medication:

Dose: Dose:

Frequency: Frequency:

Time: Time:

Medication: Medication:

Dose: Dose:

Frequency: Frequency:

Time: Time:

| Sunday | Monday | Tuesday | Wednesday |

MEDICATION TRACKING

Thursday	Friday	Saturday	Reflections

How can I simplify my to-do list?

SYMPTOM TRACKING

Sunday	Monday	Tuesday	Wednesday

MEDICATION TRACKING

Thursday	Friday	Saturday	Reflections

How can I prioritize sleep this week?

SYMPTOM TRACKING

Sunday	Monday	Tuesday	Wednesday

MEDICATION TRACKING

Thursday	Friday	Saturday	Reflections

What reminds me of my purpose in caregiving?

SYMPTOM TRACKING

Sunday	Monday	Tuesday	Wednesday

MEDICATION TRACKING

Thursday	Friday	Saturday	Reflections

How can I make next week more manageable?

SYMPTOM TRACKING

| Sunday | Monday | Tuesday | Wednesday |

MEDICATION TRACKING

Thursday	Friday	Saturday	Reflections

Psalm 55:22 - "Cast your burden on the Lord, And He shall sustain you; He shall never permit the righteous to be moved."

SYMPTOM TRACKING

Month of:

Sunday	Monday	Tuesday	Wednesday	Thursday	Friday	Saturday

Notes:

At a Glance:

MEDICAL APPOINTMENTS

- [ ]
- [ ]
- [ ]
- [ ]
- [ ]
- [ ]
- [ ]
- [ ]
- [ ]
- [ ]
- [ ]

EVENTS

PERSCRIPTIONS AND SUPPLIES

- [ ]
- [ ]
- [ ]
- [ ]
- [ ]
- [ ]
- [ ]
- [ ]
- [ ]
- [ ]
- [ ]

NEEDS

TO-DO

Caregiver Self-Care

What's one thing I'm looking forward to?

What small step can I take toward better health?

When you see the butterflies, take time for self care.

What is one way I felt God's guidance this week?

Philippians 4:6-7 - "...let your requests be made known to God; and the peace of God, which surpasses all understanding, will guard your hearts and minds through Christ Jesus."

What positive habits can I continue building?

Medication Map

Medication: Medication:

Dose: Dose:

Frequency: Frequency:

Time: Time:

Medication: Medication:

Dose: Dose:

Frequency: Frequency:

Time: Time:

Medication: Medication:

Dose: Dose:

Frequency: Frequency:

Time: Time:

Medication: Medication:

Dose: Dose:

Frequency: Frequency:

Time: Time:

Medication: Medication:

Dose: Dose:

Frequency: Frequency:

Time: Time:

| Sunday | Monday | Tuesday | Wednesday |

MEDICATION TRACKING

Thursday	Friday	Saturday	Reflections
			What's one thing I'm looking forward to?

SYMPTOM TRACKING

Sunday	Monday	Tuesday	Wednesday

MEDICATION TRACKING

Thursday	Friday	Saturday	Reflections
			What small step can I take toward better health?

SYMPTOM TRACKING

| Sunday | Monday | Tuesday | Wednesday |

MEDICATION TRACKING

Thursday	Friday	Saturday	Reflections

What is one way I felt God's guidance this week?

SYMPTOM TRACKING

| Sunday | Monday | Tuesday | Wednesday |

MEDICATION TRACKING

Thursday	Friday	Saturday	Reflections

What positive habits can I continue building?

SYMPTOM TRACKING

Sunday	Monday	Tuesday	Wednesday

MEDICATION TRACKING

Thursday

Friday

Saturday

Reflections

Philippians 4:6-7- "...let your requests be made known to God; and the peace of God, which surpasses all understanding, will guard your hearts and minds through Christ Jesus."

SYMPTOM TRACKING

Month of:

Sunday	Monday	Tuesday	Wednesday	Thursday	Friday	Saturday

Notes:

At a Glance:

MEDICAL APPOINTMENTS

- [ ] _____
- [ ] _____
- [ ] _____
- [ ] _____
- [ ] _____
- [ ] _____
- [ ] _____
- [ ] _____
- [ ] _____
- [ ] _____
- [ ] _____

EVENTS

_____
_____
_____
_____
_____

NEEDS

PERSCRIPTIONS AND SUPPLIES

- [ ] _____
- [ ] _____
- [ ] _____
- [ ] _____
- [ ] _____
- [ ] _____
- [ ] _____
- [ ] _____
- [ ] _____
- [ ] _____
- [ ] _____

TO-DO

Caregiver Self-Care

What can I do to feel lighter emotionally?

How can I create a calming space for myself?

When you see the butterflies, take time for self care.

How can I seek grace in challenging moments?

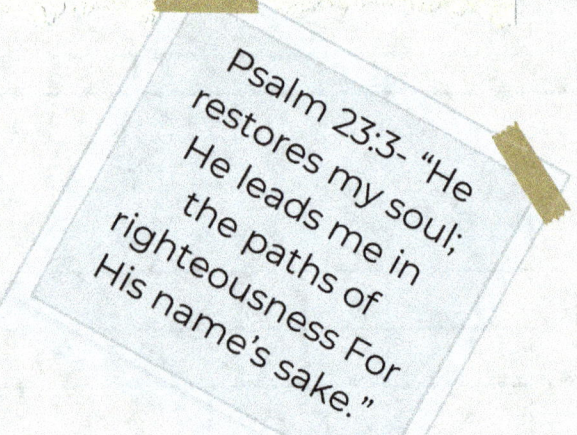

Psalm 23:3- "He restores my soul; He leads me in the paths of righteousness For His name's sake."

What is one thing I can let go of to feel freer?

Medication Map

Medication:	Medication:
Dose:	Dose:
Frequency:	Frequency:
Time:	Time:
Medication:	Medication:
Dose:	Dose:
Frequency:	Frequency:
Time:	Time:
Medication:	Medication:
Dose:	Dose:
Frequency:	Frequency:
Time:	Time:
Medication:	Medication:
Dose:	Dose:
Frequency:	Frequency:
Time:	Time:
Medication:	Medication:
Dose:	Dose:
Frequency:	Frequency:
Time:	Time:

Sunday	Monday	Tuesday	Wednesday

MEDICATION TRACKING

Thursday	Friday	Saturday	Reflections

What can I do to feel lighter emotionally?

SYMPTOM TRACKING

Sunday	Monday	Tuesday	Wednesday

MEDICATION TRACKING

| Thursday | Friday | Saturday | Reflections |

How can I create a calming space for myself?

SYMPTOM TRACKING

| Sunday | Monday | Tuesday | Wednesday |

MEDICATION TRACKING

Thursday   Friday   Saturday   Reflections

How can I seek grace in challenging moments?

SYMPTOM TRACKING

Sunday	Monday	Tuesday	Wednesday

MEDICATION TRACKING

Thursday | Friday | Saturday | Reflections

What is one thing I can let go of to feel freer?

SYMPTOM TRACKING

Sunday | Monday | Tuesday | Wednesday

MEDICATION TRACKING

Thursday	Friday	Saturday	Reflections
			Psalm 23:3- "He restores my soul; He leads me in the paths of righteousness For His name's sake."

SYMPTOM TRACKING

Month of:

Sunday	Monday	Tuesday	Wednesday	Thursday	Friday	Saturday

Notes:

At a Glance:

MEDICAL APPOINTMENTS

- [ ] _____
- [ ] _____
- [ ] _____
- [ ] _____
- [ ] _____
- [ ] _____
- [ ] _____
- [ ] _____
- [ ] _____
- [ ] _____
- [ ] _____

PERSCRIPTIONS AND SUPPLIES

- [ ] _____
- [ ] _____
- [ ] _____
- [ ] _____
- [ ] _____
- [ ] _____
- [ ] _____
- [ ] _____
- [ ] _____
- [ ] _____
- [ ] _____

EVENTS

_____
_____
_____
_____
_____
_____

NEEDS

TO-DO

Caregiver Self-Care

How can I challenge a negative thought?

What physical discomfort can I address this week?

When you see the butterflies, take time for self care.

How can I let go and trust more deeply?

Ephesians 6:10- "Finally, my brethren, be strong in the Lord and in the power of His might."

How can I find joy in the little things?

Medication Map

Medication: Medication:

Dose: Dose:

Frequency: Frequency:

Time: Time:

Medication: Medication:

Dose: Dose:

Frequency: Frequency:

Time: Time:

Medication: Medication:

Dose: Dose:

Frequency: Frequency:

Time: Time:

Medication: Medication:

Dose: Dose:

Frequency: Frequency:

Time: Time:

Medication: Medication:

Dose: Dose:

Frequency: Frequency:

Time: Time:

| Sunday | Monday | Tuesday | Wednesday |

MEDICATION TRACKING

Thursday	Friday	Saturday	Reflections

How can I challenge a negative thought?

SYMPTOM TRACKING

| Sunday | Monday | Tuesday | Wednesday |

MEDICATION TRACKING

Thursday	Friday	Saturday	Reflections
			What physical discomfort can I address this week?

SYMPTOM TRACKING

Sunday	Monday	Tuesday	Wednesday

MEDICATION TRACKING

Thursday	Friday	Saturday	Reflections

How can I let go and trust more deeply?

SYMPTOM TRACKING

Sunday	Monday	Tuesday	Wednesday

MEDICATION TRACKING

Thursday	Friday	Saturday	Reflections

How can I find joy in the little things?

SYMPTOM TRACKING

Sunday	Monday	Tuesday	Wednesday

MEDICATION TRACKING

Thursday	Friday	Saturday	Reflections

Ephesians 6:10- "Finally, my brethren, be strong in the Lord and in the power of His might."

SYMPTOM TRACKING

Notes

Notes

Notes

Notes

Notes

Notes

Notes

All Scripture quotations are taken from the New King James Version (NKJV). Copyright © 1982 by Thomas Nelson. Used by permission. All rights reserved.

www.ingramcontent.com/pod-product-compliance
Lightning Source LLC
Chambersburg PA
CBHW051352070526

44584CB00025B/3728